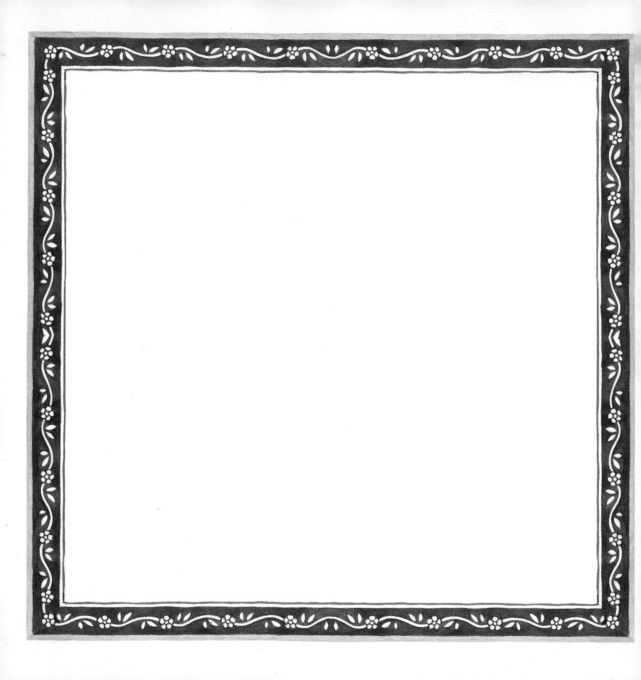

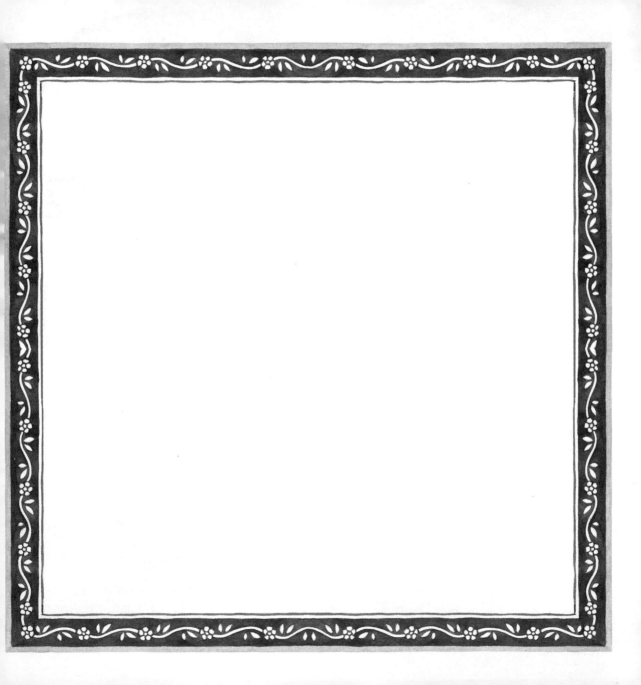

A CUP *of* TEA

A Cup *of* Tea

Treasures for Teatime

Collected by
Geraldene Holt

PAVILION

First published in Great Britain in 1991 by
Pavilion Books Limited
London House, Great Eastern Wharf, Parkgate Road, London SW11 4NQ

Compilation and introduction copyright © 1991 Geraldene Holt
Teacup illustrations copyright © 1991 Minton Limited
Border illustrations copyright © 1991 Maria Rogers

Designed by Mathewson Bull

ISBN 1 85793 2307

Printed and bound in Spain

4 6 8 10 9 7 5 3

This book may be ordered by post direct from the publisher.
Please contact the Marketing Department.
But try your bookshop first.

CONTENTS

INTRODUCTION

I CAME TO tea drinking relatively late in life. Not until I left home at around 18 years of age did I start to taste what I now regard as a life-preserving liquid that can be imbibed at any time of the day or night with only good effect.

Who knows how we form our gastronomic allegiances. I do know, though, that when I was a child my mother discouraged me from drinking tea. She maintained that children should drink milk – or water – and that cups of Indian tea would simply stunt the growth of my brothers and myself. At the time, in post-war Britain, tea was rationed and every adult was allowed a few scarce ounces of leaf-tea each week.

I imagine that my tea-drinking parents, in despair at the deprivations of the time, drank every drop of the precious liquid themselves. And I must admit that on the few occasions when I was able to sip a little of the dark brown brew, I wanted to spit it out straight away, because it tasted so bitter. And so tea became, for me, an adult drink, something to be experimented with when I had a room and a teapot of my own. Quite quickly I discovered that strong Indian tea made my face flushed and that I preferred the subtle, delicate flavour of China and Ceylon teas. I enjoyed – and still do – a smoky Lapsang Souchong or a scented Orange Pekoe or a flower-flecked Jasmine Tea. Although I still prefer tea of medium strength, I know now that there is no liquid in the world to compare with freshly-brewed strong Darjeeling tea served with milk in your favourite cup. When you are tired or stressed, a large steaming cup of tea is the most reviving liquid you can be offered.

Such cups that cheer are usually downed late at night or in the grey light of early morning when food is far from one's mind. Later in the day, tea drinking is different.

Nearly every afternoon of my married life, at sometime between half past three and five o'clock I have served tea – to my family if they are home, or to friends, or to myself. I select a tea-tray, either dark polished mahogany or a lightweight papier-mâché painted tray, and if my mother is staying I add an embroidered tray cloth. I choose a set of pretty teacups, and add a jug of milk and a tea strainer, and then a pot of tea, to sustain me during an afternoon of writing. If I am gardening, I take the tea outside. Usually I add to the tray one of my home-made cakes: a dark, rich chocolate cake or tiny iced petit fours, petticoat tails of Scottish shortbread or almond macaroons. Or perhaps some hazelnut meringues or shell-shaped golden madeleines. In the winter we like a plate of hot buttery crumpets, in summer some cucumber sandwiches. And in no time at all, a simple tray of tea has become the magical English meal known as afternoon tea.

No-one is quite sure when afternoon tea was introduced into England. Some authorities claim that Anna, Duchess of Bedford devised the custom around 1840. She is reputed to have said that afternoon tea served with a little light refreshment saved her from 'that sinking feeling' that overcame her between luncheon and dinner. In France, however, afternoon tea had arrived over a century earlier. In a letter to a friend, the indefatigable Madame de Sevigné (1626-96) referred to *'le thé de cinq heures'* and mentions her surprise at discovering that some people take milk in their tea.

Although the Chinese discovered tea as a drink nearly 5,000 years ago, tea arrived in Europe via Portugal and Holland only during the seventeenth century. From his City of London coffee house in 1658, Thomas Garway advertised 'the excellent and by all physitians approved China drink, called by the Chineans Tcha, by other nations Tay, alias Tee'.

13

Tea is simply an infusion made with the leaves from the evergreen plant, Camellia sinensis. The plant is now widely grown in India, Ceylon and east Africa as well as in its homeland, China. The dark green glossy leaves are processed in a variety of ways to produce teas with different flavours. Green tea, like Gunpowder, is produced by allowing the leaves to dry or wither in the open air, then the leaves are steamed, rolled and dried. Black teas such as Assam and Darjeeling, are produced from picked and withered leaves which are then broken to release the enzymes, the leaves are allowed to ferment for 3½-4½ hours before being dried in a warm air oven. By arresting the fermenting process for a black tea, a semi-fermented tea is produced with a different flavour.

It may be that most of us belong to either of two groups: those who never mind – or even notice – whether their teacup matches its saucer, and the others for whom tea drinking can be spoiled when deprived of the balance and harmony, and the happy feel of the right cup atop the right saucer. Those casual tea drinkers of the former group can never understand the displeasure verging on pain that one feels when drinking from a mismatched cup and saucer. Even those around me who do not share my preference, usually take the trouble to ensure that my cup always has its rightful saucer.

14

Of course, life would be simpler if I owned less crockery, but I can't imagine such a situation. I am an inveterate collector of teacups, old and new, and I am only able to continue with this crazy habit by now and again giving away some of my less favoured specimens.

But there are no cups and saucers made by myself on my shelves. The odd mug or two has survived, usually with a kiln flaw or the result of a glaze experiment – but there are no teacups. In my time as a potter I made very few cups and saucers and those I gave away because I prefer to drink out of porcelain, bone china or earthenware. I worked in stoneware and so, instead of cups, I made teapots, which every domestic potter regards as a satisfying challenge, and the kind of pot by which one might be judged. My half dozen stoneware teapots that have survived, I use with loving care and a keen sense of how much has happened since I made them.

Yet how much more time has passed since the beautiful teacups in this book were created. These charming cups decorated with patterns that emphasise and flatter the shape of both the cup and the saucer seem as fresh and delightful as when they were first painted.

When I visited the Minton Museum in Stoke-on-Trent I was fortunate in being allowed to turn the pages of the earliest Minton pattern book; it was in use from about 1800-1816, which is known as the first period. The book is quite small, hardly bigger than 6 inches square but within its tattered leather covers are over one hundred and forty numbered designs – pieces of first period Minton are only identifiable by their pattern number. Each page carries a watercolour portrait of a teabowl on its saucer and the freshness of the colours and the finesse of the brushwork quite take your breath away.

Tiny sprigs of flowers perhaps inspired by the dress muslins of the day, swags of leaves and garlands of rosebuds, exotic birds and brightly-hued harlequins glow on the page, all of them executed with infinite care. I am struck by the immediate appeal of each pattern, and how as soon as you have decided on a favourite you turn the page and another wins you over. Many of the designs are gilded – gold is represented by yellow paint. Some of the patterns are rich and complicated, others are deceptively simple. One design is composed of just four elements: a leaf, a petal, a dot and a line, yet they are so artfully arranged that the pattern has such life and strength that it flows around the edge of the cup and the rim of the saucer in a ceaseless movement. And I find myself wondering who painted these pictures, who created the designs and what inspired them?

What we do know is that Thomas Minton was born in Shropshire in 1765. He trained as an engraver in a Caughley porcelain factory and then practised his trade in London. In 1789 he married and came to Stoke-on-Trent where his designing and engraving skills were in high demand in the potteries of the area. Encouraged by the response to his work, Minton, in partnership with two friends, founded his own pottery in the town in 1793. Initially he produced the popular blue and white printed ware of the time. Then around 1798 Thomas Minton introduced bone china, made from Cornish china clay and bone ash, which became a hugely successful alternative to porcelain.

By 1810 the factory was producing a very wide range of ware. Customers chose their china from samples and a pattern book at their local retailer. A Minton tea-set of the time comprised a teapot and oval stand, sugar box, milk ewer and slop bowl. The twelve cups (the earlier tea bowls were soon ousted by the more convenient teacup with its pretty ring handle) were sold with matching saucers and coffee cans – the saucers were used with either. Two bread and butter plates completed the tea-set.

Imagine the thrill of unpacking a new Minton tea-set, and the excitement of that first brew of tea – made in the drawing room with tea blended by the hostess from the several kinds stored in her locked wooden tea caddy. I like to ponder on those days in the early nineteenth century when cups of the designs in this book were made and sold, and given and treasured. I think about the houses and the drawing rooms, the kitchens and the cupboards where they were kept. And the people who cared for them and what they thought and felt and loved and lost. For as a wise French writer once said, 'the reconstitution of the past is a delicate pleasure of which one should not be deprived'.

Geraldene Holt
1990

№ 104

A GIFT FROM THE EAST

'TEA IS LIKE the East he grows in,
A great yellow mandarin
With urbanity of manner
And unconsciousness of sin.'

G. K. CHESTERTON
The Song of Right and Wrong

'THE PHILOSOPHY OF Tea is not mere aestheticism in the ordinary acceptance of the term, for it expresses conjointly with ethics and religion our whole point of view about man and nature. It is hygiene, for it enforces cleanliness; it is economics, for it shows comfort in simplicity rather than in the complex and costly; it is moral geometry, inasmuch as it defines our sense of proportion to the universe. It represents the true spirit of eastern democracy by making all its votaries aristocrats in taste.'

OKAKURA KAKUZO
The Book of Tea

N.º 127

Nº 105

23

'THERE IS A story that Confucius, in order to induce the Chinese to boil their drinking water, invented the tea made from the leaves of the "Thea bohea" or "Thea viridis". Whatever the origin of the practice, all drinks made from brewing fragrant leaves or flowers in hot water are known as teas.'

HELEN MORGENTHAU FOX
Gardening with Herbs for Flavor and Fragrance

'THE FIRST ORDER of business in most homes is the setting up of the samovar. Some live charcoal from the *kangri* is thrown down its chimney. Water is poured into its belly and after much blowing, huffing and puffing on the coals, it finally begins to heat. Once it is boiling, loose green tea, (called "Bombay tea" for some reason, even though it is more like teas drunk in China and Tibet) is sprinkled in and a little sugar, if the family wants it. Those who can afford it crush some cardamom and almonds in a mortar and put them in as well. This is *kahva*. It will be drunk for breakfast and then sipped through the course of the day until the last person beds down again in a huddle of quilts and shawls.'

MADHUR JAFFREY
A Taste of India

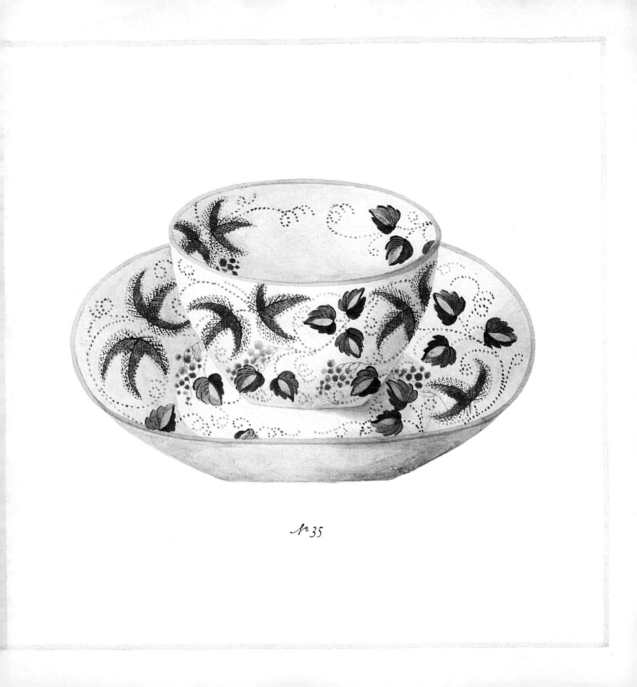

N° 35

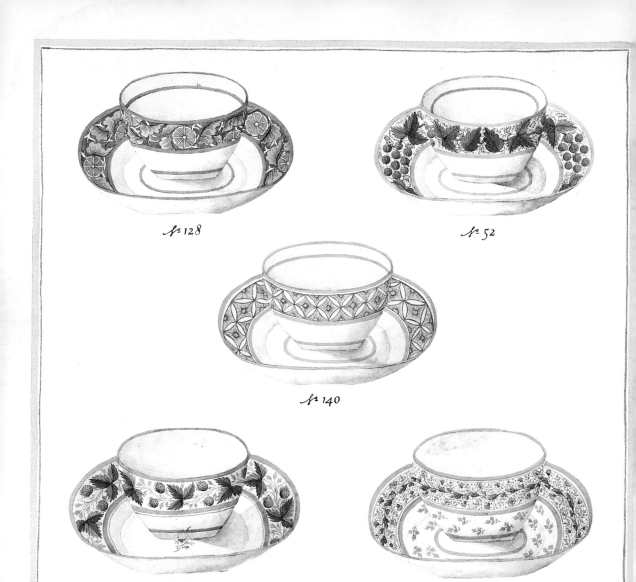

N.º 128

N.º 52

N.º 140

N.º 60

N.º 73

Almond and Lemon Shortbread

CREAM 8TBSP/4OZ butter with 4tbsp/2oz superfine/caster sugar and ½tsp finely grated zest of lemon. Gradually work in ⅔ cup/2oz ground almonds and 1 cup/5oz plain (all purpose) flour until the mixture forms a soft dough. Divide in half and roll or press each piece into a 6-7 inch round of shortbread. Transfer to a lightly-buttered baking sheet and sprinkle ¼ cup/½oz flaked almonds over the shortbread. Decorate the edges by pressing with your fingertips all the way round to give a fluted finish. Mark each shortbread into 6 pieces. Bake in an oven heated to 325°F/170°C/gas mark 3 for 25/30 minutes until the shortbread is just changing colour at the edges. Cool for 5 minutes on the baking sheet, then transfer to a wire rack to cool and sprinkle with a little sugar.

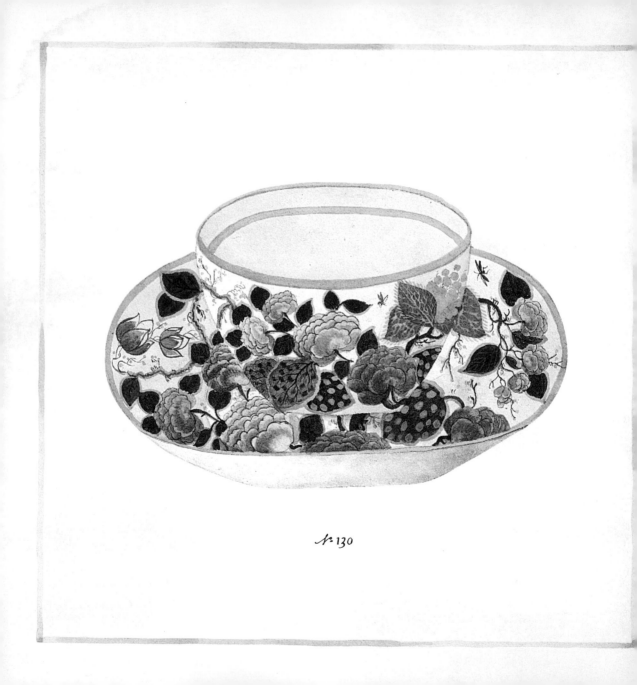

Nº 130

THE SPIRIT OF TEA

'I MYSELF PREFER a tea made partly of Indian tea, partly from the dry flowerheads of the American wild Bergamot or Oswego Tea, the "Monarda didyma" which now has so many garden forms; and being conservative, I prefer my flowerheads from the good, honest, ragged, fragrant, "scarlet" Monarda, the wild form (which in America is much attended by hummingbirds).

Ordinary tea goes into the pot in the ordinary quantity, with one or two of the dry heads (if you take them straight from the garden, you may, of course, be risking Earwig Tea); and then water is added in the ordinary way. You can say the resulting liquor tastes like one of the scented Chinese teas.'

GEOFFREY GRIGSON
A Herbal of All Sorts

'LIKE ART, TEA has its periods and its schools, its evolution may be roughly divided into three main stages; The Boiled Tea, The Whipped Tea and The Steeped Tea. We modern belong to the last school. These several methods of appreciating the beverage are indicative of the spirit of the age in which they prevailed.'

OKAKURA KAKUZA
The Book of Tea

N.º 62

Nᵒ 133

'TEA, ALTHOUGH an oriental,
Is a gentleman at least;
Cocoa is a cad and coward,
Cocoa is a vulgar beast.'

G. K. CHESTERTON
The Song of Right and Wrong

34

'GRANDMOTHER, BORN IN County Tyrone, believed as a good Irishwoman that there were only three kinds of tea fit to drink, none of them store-bought. The first quality was kept, sensibly enough, in China. The second picking was sent directly to Ireland. The third and lowest grade went, of course, to the benighted British. And all the tea used in our house came once a year, in one or two beautiful soldered tin boxes, from Dublin. Then only would we know it be second to what the Dowager Empress of China was drinking, while the other Old Lady in Buckingham Palace sipped our dregs, as served her right.'

M. F. K. FISHER
The Tea Lovers' Treasury

N.° 14

N.° 91

N.° 23

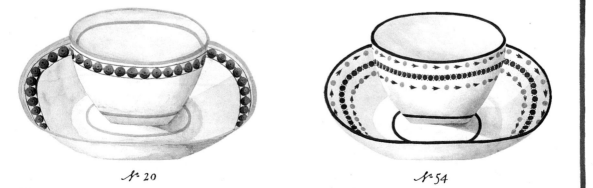

N.° 20

N.° 54

N.º 112

A CIVILIZING INFLUENCE

'AND SUDDENLY THE memory revealed itself. The taste was that of the little piece of madeleine which on Sunday mornings at Combray (because on those mornings I did not go out before mass), when I went to say good morning to her in her bedroom, my aunt Leonie used to give me, dipping it first in her own cup of tea or tisane.'

MARCEL PROUST
A la Recherche du Temps Perdu

Madeleines

CREAM 4TBSP/2OZ of softened butter with ⅔ cup/5oz super-
fine/caster sugar and the finely-grated zest of ½ lemon. Beat in
the yolks of 3 eggs with 1 teaspoon of orange-flower water.
Fold in 3 stiffly-whisked whites of egg alternately with ¾ cup/
4oz sieved all purpose/plain flour. Brush clarified butter into
the shell-shaped moulds of a madeleine tin. Place 1 rounded
teaspoon of the mixture in each shell shape and smooth fairly
level. Bake the cakes in an oven heated to 350°F/180°C/gas
mark 4 for about 15 minutes or until the little cakes are just
starting to shrink from the tin. Cool the cakes in the tin
for 1 minute then transfer to a wire rack to cool. Makes 24
madeleine cakes.

N.º 126

N.º 139

'BANKING IS BUSINESS, oil is industry, tea and coffee are trades, but the tea trade in particular has always had a special aristocratic position in the world of buying and selling.'

EDWARD BRAMAH
Tea and Coffee:
a Modern View of 300 Years of Tradition

'NOWHERE IS THE English genius for domesticity more notably evidenced than in the festival of afternoon tea.'

GEORGE GISSING

The Private Papers of Henry Ryecroft

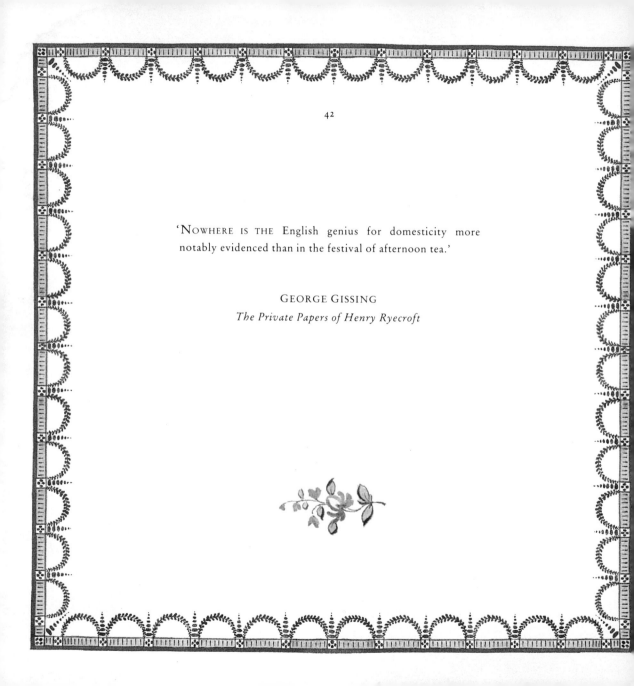

N.º 2

N.º 74

N.º 8

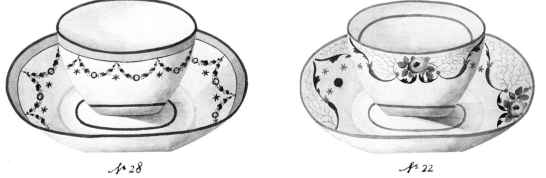

N.º 28

N.º 22

N. 123

TEA IN AMERICA

THE BOSTON TEA PARTY on 16 December 1773 presaged the American War of Independence and the founding of the United States of America. Tea that arrived in other ports along the eastern seaboard was also under threat, in the port of Greenwich, then the largest town in New Jersey, tea intended for Philadelphia was destroyed.

'Citizens of the quiet Jersey village hurried to their doors on that night, December 22, 1773, as shrill war whoops sounded and a lurid glow lit the low-lying clouds. The hated tea, together with the chests that contained it, was burning in the middle of Market Square, and none there were who dared to stay the weird figures in paint and feathers who burned it.'

W. H. UKERS
All About Tea

'CAN POSTERITY BELIEVE that the constitutional liberties of North America were on the point of being given up for Tea? Is this exotic Plant necessary to Life? But if we must through Custom have some warm Tea once or twice a day, why may we not exchange this slow poison which not only destroys our Constitutions but endangers our Liberties and drains our Country of so many thousands of Pounds a Year for Teas of our own American Plants, many of which may be found pleasant to the taste, and very salutary, according to our various constitutions ... Sweet marjoram and a little mint; mother of thyme, a little hyssop; sage and balm leaves, joined with a little lemon juice; rosemary and lavender; a very few small twigs of White Oak dried in the Sun with two leaves and a Half a Sweet Myrtle; Clover with a little Chamomile; Twigs of Blackcurrant Bushes; Red Rose Bush leaves and Cinquefoil; Mistletoe and English Wild Valerian ...'

From an article in the *Virginia Gazette,*
Williamsburg, 1774

Nᵒ 101

Nº 144

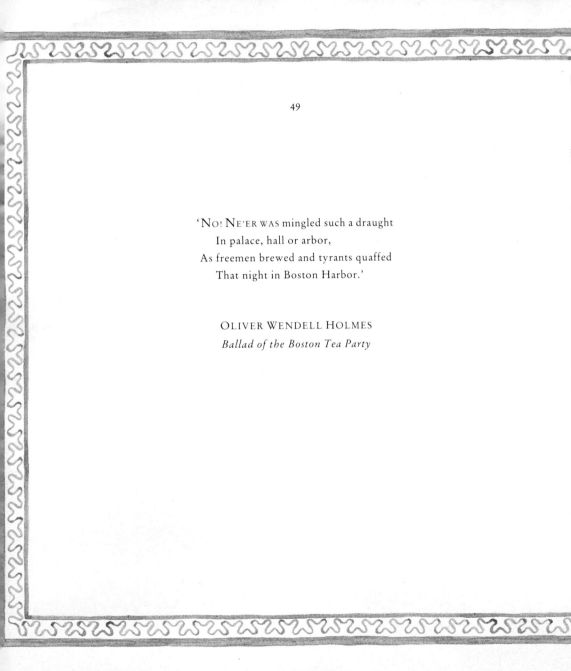

'No! Ne'er was mingled such a draught
In palace, hall or arbor,
As freemen brewed and tyrants quaffed
That night in Boston Harbor.'

OLIVER WENDELL HOLMES
Ballad of the Boston Tea Party

Brandy Snap Biscuits

IN A SAUCEPAN gently heat 8tbsp/4oz butter, ½ cup/4oz demerara sugar and 6tbsp/4oz golden syrup until melted, then stir until the sugar has dissolved. Remove from the heat and mix in 1tsp lemon juice and 1tsp brandy. Stir in ¾ cup/4oz all purpose/plain flour sifted with 1tsp ground ginger until smooth. Place teaspoons of the mixture, well-spaced, on greased non-stick baking sheets. Bake in an oven heated to 325°F/170°C/gas mark 3 for 8-10 minutes until golden brown. Remove from the oven and straight away gently wrap each biscuit around the handle of a wooden spoon. If necessary, the biscuits can be softened by placing the tray back in the oven for 1-2 minutes. When the biscuits are cool, slide them free of the handles. Serve the biscuits plain or filled with whipped cream. Makes 30 brandy snaps.

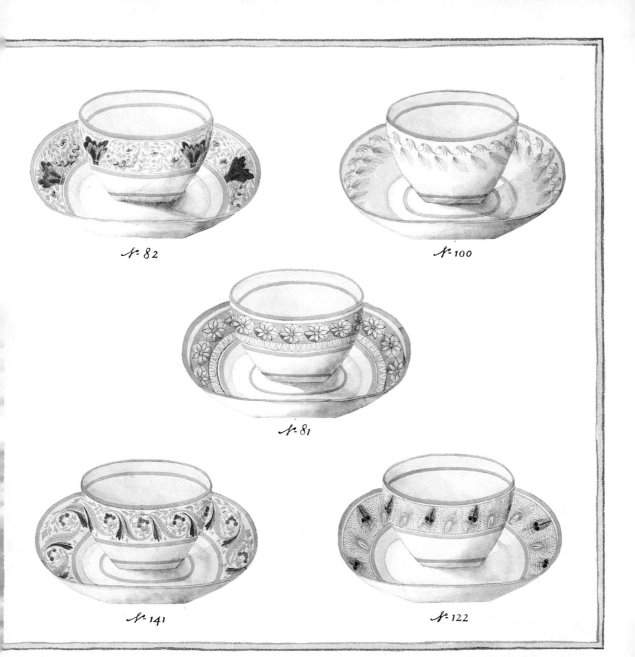

N.° 82   N.° 100

N.° 81

N.° 141   N.° 122

№ 86

TEA, THE CURE-ALL

'IF YOU ARE COLD, tea will warm you;
if you are too heated, it will cool you;
if you are depressed, it will cheer you;
if you are exhausted, it will calm you.'

WILLIAM GLADSTONE

'WHAT PART OF confidante has that poor teapot played ever since the kindly plant was introduced among us. Why myriads of women have cried over it, to be sure! What sickbeds it has smoked by! What fevered lips have received refreshment from it! Nature meant very kindly by women when she made the tea plant; and with a little thought, what a series of pictures and groups the fancy may conjure up and assemble round the teapot and cup.'

WILLIAM MAKEPEACE THACKERAY
Pendennis

Nº 85

N.º 59

DR JOHNSON (1709-84), the famous lexicographer, described himself in *The Literary Magazine* as 'A hardened and shameless tea-drinker, who has, for twenty years diluted his meals with only the infusion of this fascinating plant; whose kettle has scarcely time to cool; who with tea amuses the evening, with tea solaces the midnight, and with tea welcomes the morning.'

Devon Honey Cake

MEASURE 6TBSP/6OZ Devon honey, 10tbsp/5oz butter, ½ cup/ 3oz light muscovado sugar and 1tbsp water into a saucepan and stir over low heat until melted. Remove from the heat and mix in 2 beaten eggs with ¾ cup/7oz sieved cake/self-raising flour. Pour the mixture into a greased and lined 7-inch diameter cake tin. Bake in an oven heated to 350°F/180°C/gas mark 4 for 40-45 minutes or until the cake is springy in the centre and the edges are just shrinking from the tin. Cool in the tin for 1 minute, then transfer to a wire rack. When the cake is still warm, mix ½ cup/2oz sieved icing sugar with 1 tablespoon clear honey and 2-3 teaspoons warm water to make a smooth icing. Trickle the icing over the cake in a lattice design and leave until set.

N.° 129

N.° 121

N.° 76

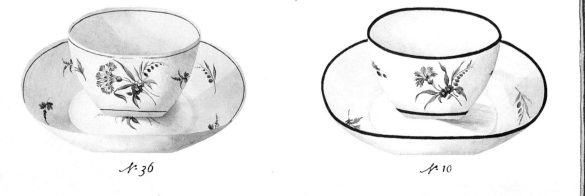

N.° 36

N.° 10

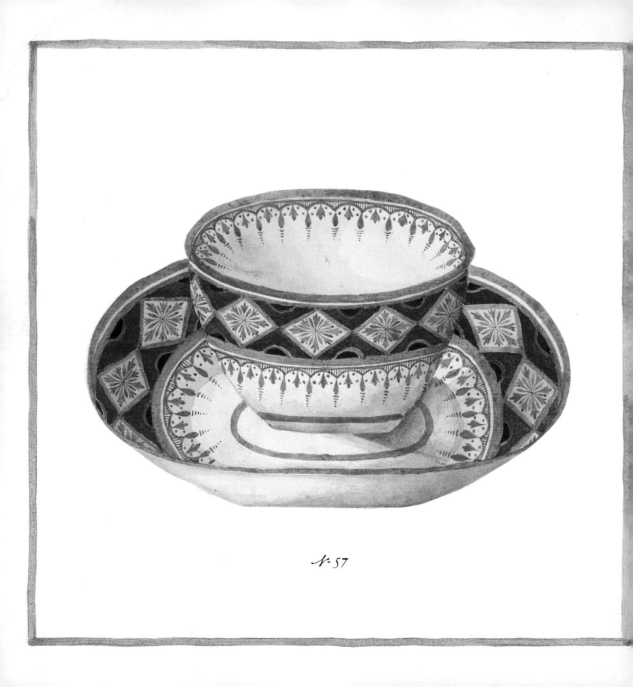

Nº 57

THE PHILOSOPHER'S BREW

' ... FOR TEA, though ridiculed by those who are naturally coarse in their nervous sensibilities, or are become so from wine-drinking, and are not susceptible of influence from so refined a stimulant, will always be the favoured beverage of the intellectual ...'

THOMAS DE QUINCEY
Confessions of an English Opium-Eater

'HERE THOU, GREAT Anna, whom three realms obey,
Dost sometimes counsel take and sometimes tea.'

ALEXANDER POPE
Referring to Queen Anne in *The Rape of the Lock*

No. 146

No. 53

'FOR HER OWN breakfast she'll project a scheme,
Nor take her tea without a strategem.'

EDWARD YOUNG
Love of Fame: The Universal Passion

Iced Tea

MEASURE 6 TEASPOONS of Darjeeling tea into a jug and pour
on 2 cups/1¾ pints of cold water. Stir well then cover and
chill for 4-6 hours. Strain the tea into a serving jug, add sugar
to taste and garnish with slices of lemon and sprigs of mint.
Serve in glasses with ice cubes. Serves 6.

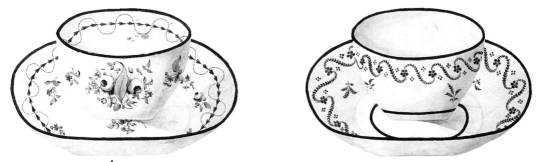

N.º 4   N.º 6

N.º 96

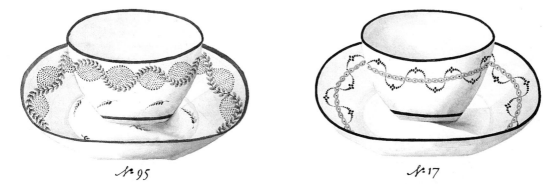

N.º 95   N.º 17

№ 77

BY THE FIRESIDE

'SURELY EVERY ONE is aware of the divine pleasures which attend a wintry fireside: candles at four o'clock, warm hearthrugs, tea, a fair tea-maker, shutters closed, curtains flowing in ample draperies to the floor, whilst the wind and rain are raging audibly without.'

THOMAS DE QUINCEY
Confessions of an English Opium-Eater

'TEA HAD COME as a deliverer to a land that called for deliverance; a land of beef and ale, of heavy eating and abundant drunkenness; of grey skies and harsh winds; of strong-nerved, stout-purposed, slow-thinking men and women. Above all, a land of sheltered homes and warm firesides – firesides that were waiting – waiting, for the bubbling kettle and the fragrant breath of tea.'

AGNES REPPLIER
To Think of Tea!

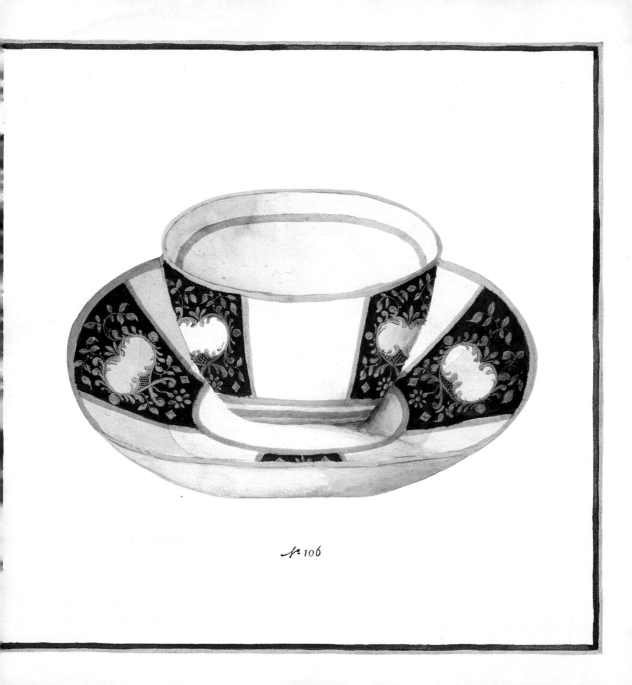

No 106

No 38

'Now stir the fire, and close the shutters fast,
Let fall the curtains, wheel the sofa round,
And while the bubbling and loud-hissing urn
Throws up a steamy column, and the cups
That cheer but not inebriate, wait on each,
So let us welcome peaceful evening in.'

WILLIAM COWPER
The Task

English Scones

SIEVE 1¾ CUPS/8oz cake/self-raising flour, 1 teaspoon of baking powder and ¼ cup/1½oz superfine/caster sugar into a mixing bowl. Rub in 4tbsp/2oz butter until the mixture resembles breadcrumbs. Mix to a soft dough with 1 egg beaten with milk to measure ¼ pint. Turn the dough on to a floured board and pat or roll out until ½ inch thick. Use a fluted 2-inch pastry cutter to cut out as many scones as possible. Lightly knead together the trimmings and cut out the rest of the scones. Place the scones on a lightly-floured baking sheet and brush the tops with a mixture of yolk of egg mixed with a little milk. Bake the scones in an oven preheated to 425°F/220°C/gas mark 7 for 12-15 minutes until the scones are well risen and golden-brown. Transfer to a wire rack to cool slightly or serve straight away with home-made strawberry jam and butter or clotted cream. Makes 12 scones.

Nº 72

Nº 26

Nº 15

Nº 107'8

Nº 99

No: 93

THE TEA HOUR

'THERE ARE FEW hours in life more agreeable than the hour dedicated to the ceremony known as afternoon tea.'

HENRY JAMES
The Portrait of a Lady

'THE RITUAL OF the English tea-time was brought to perfection by the late Queen Mary, for whom it was the favourite time of day. Everything had to be fully ready by 4 p.m. punctually, with sandwiches, cakes and biscuits invitingly set out on gleaming silver dishes upon a smoothly-running trolley. The teapot, cream jug, hot-water jug and sugar bowl were always the same antique silver service which had been a favourite of Queen Victoria . . . Queen Mary would take over and meticulously measure out her favourite Indian tea from a jade tea-caddy she kept locked in a cupboard. Then she would pour on the boiling water and complete the tea-making ritual by snuffing out the spirit stove before sitting back for the footmen to pour tea and hand round sandwiches and cakes. But before Queen Mary gave the signal for this to begin she would always let exactly three minutes elapse from the moment she poured hot water on to the leaves so that the tea would be perfectly brewed.'

CHARLES OLIVER
Dinner at Buckingham Palace

N.º 56

N.º 70

'STANDS THE CHURCH clock at ten to three?
And is there honey still for tea?'

RUPERT BROOKE
The Old Vicarage, Grantchester

'THERE IS VERY little art in making good tea; if the water is boiling, and there is no sparing of the fragrant leaf, the beverage will almost invariably be good. The old-fashioned plan of allowing a teaspoonful to each person, and one over, is still practised. Warm the teapot with boiling water; let it remain for two or three minutes for the vessel to become thoroughly hot, then pour it away. Put in the tea, pour in ½ to ¾ pint of 'boiling' water, close the lid, and let it stand for the tea to draw from 5 to 10 minutes; then fill up the pot with water. The tea will be quite spoiled unless made with water that is 'actually boiling', as the leaves will not open, and the flavour will not be extracted from them; the beverage will consequently be colourless and tasteless – in fact, nothing but tepid water.'

MRS ISABELLA BEETON
The Book of Household Management

N.º 78

N.º 79

N.º 80

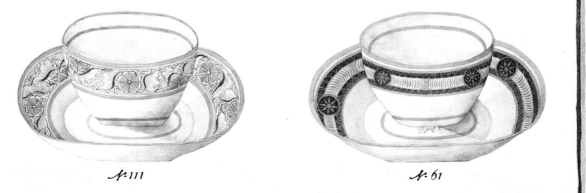

N.º 111

N.º 61

№ 124

LIFE WITHOUT TEA

'INDEED, MADAM, YOUR Ladyship is very sparing of your tea;
I protest the last I took was no more than water bewitched.'

JONATHAN SWIFT

'THANK GOD FOR tea! What would the world do without tea?
How did it exist? I am glad I was not born before tea.'

THE REVEREND SIDNEY SMITH

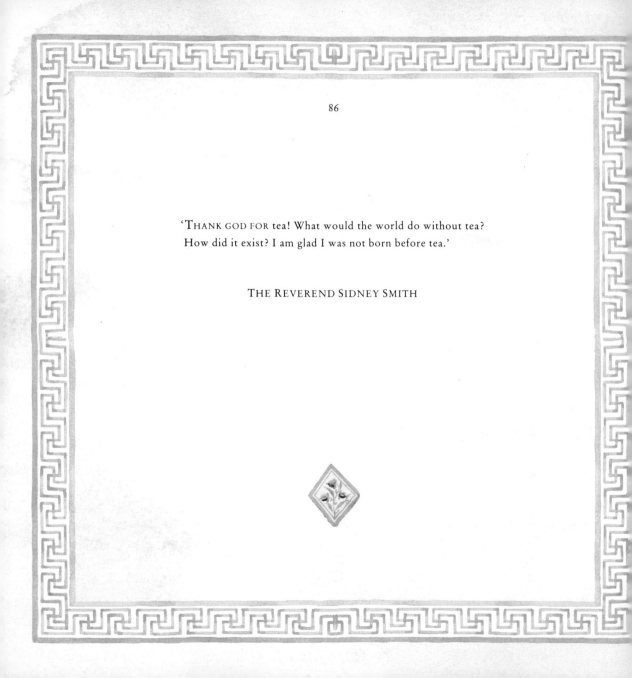

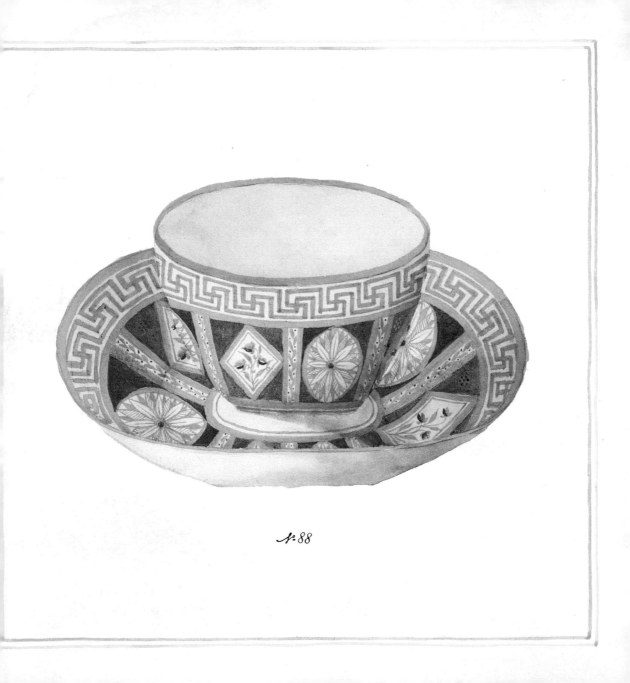

N.º 88

N.º 98

'LOOK HERE, STEWARD, if this is coffee, I want tea; but if this is tea, then I wish for coffee.'

Cartoon in *Punch*, 1902

'WE HAD A KETTLE, we let it leak;
  Our not replacing it made it worse,
We haven't had any tea for a week ...
  The bottom is out of the Universe!'

RUDYARD KIPLING
Natural Theology

Nº 97

ACKNOWLEDGEMENTS

The extract from GARDENING WITH HERBS FOR FLAVOR AND FRAGRANCE by Helen Morgenthau Fox is reprinted by permission of Dover Publications Inc., New York; the extract from A TASTE OF INDIA by Madhur Jaffrey is reprinted by permission of the author and Pavilion Books Ltd., London; the extract from A HERBAL OF ALL SORTS by Geoffrey Grigson is reprinted by permission of the author, Phoenix House Ltd., London and David Higham Associates Ltd., London; the extract from THE TEA LOVERS' TREASURY by M.F.K. Fisher, copyright 1988 Chevron Chemical Company, published by 101 Productions and distributed by Ortho Information Services is reprinted by permission; the extract from ALL ABOUT TEA by W.H. Ukers is reprinted by permission of TEA AND COFFEE Trade Journal; the extract from TO THINK OF TEA! by Agnes Repplier is reprinted by permission of Houghton Mifflin Company, Boston; the extract 'Dinner at Buckingham Palace' from THE TEA LOVERS' TREASURY, copyright 1988 Chevron Chemical Company, published by 101 Publications and distributed by Ortho Information Services is reprinted by permission.

Every effort has been made to trace the holders of copyright material used in this anthology. We apologise for any omissions in this respect, and on notification we undertake to make the appropriate acknowledgement in subsequent editions.